DISCARD

BEAUTIFUL BIRDS

ALVIN SILVERSTEIN · VIRGINIA SILVERSTEIN · LAURA SILVERSTEIN NUNN

TWENTY-FIRST CENTURY BOOKS
BROOKFIELD, CONNECTICUT

Cover photograph courtesy of Photo Researchers, Inc. (© Carolyn A. McKeone)

Photographs courtesy of Animals Animals: pp. 6 (© Gerard Lacz), 10 (© Robert Maier),
18 (© J. &. P. Wegner), 26 (© Robert Maier), 42 (© Erwin & Peggy Bauer); Photo Researchers,
Inc.: pp. 14 (© Carolyn A. McKeone), 22 (© Dana Hyde), 30 (© Alan L. Detrick);
Bruce Coleman, Inc.: p. 34 (© Hans Reinhard);
Peter Arnold, Inc.: 38 (© Manfred Danegger)

Library of Congress Cataloging-in-Publication Data

Silverstein, Alvin.
Beautiful birds / Alvin Silverstein, Virginia Silverstein, Laura
Silverstein Nunn.
p. cm. — (What a pet!)
Summary: Looks at the birds most commonly owned as pets, including
canaries, chickens, and pigeons, and offers advice on their care,
feeding, and breeding.
Includes bibliographical references (p.   ) and index.
ISBN 0-7613-2513-1 (lib. bdg.)
1. Cage birds—Juvenile literature. [1. Birds as pets. 2. Pets.] I.
Silverstein, Virginia B. II. Nunn, Laura Silverstein. III. Title.

SF461.35 .S56 2003
636.6'8—dc21

2002151757

Published by Twenty-First Century Books
A Division of The Millbrook Press, Inc.
2 Old New Milford Road
Brookfield, CT 06804
www.millbrookpress.com

CONTENTS

What Is a Bird?

People have always been fascinated with birds and their ability to fly. All birds have wings, but not all birds can fly. An ostrich, for example, walks or runs, using its wings to keep its balance. A penguin uses its wings like flippers when it swims.

Most birds do fly, though, and their bodies have special adaptations for flight. Air can flow smoothly over their sleek bodies without much resistance. The front legs of their reptile ancestors evolved into wings to lift birds off the ground and keep them airborne. Powerful chest muscles move the wings, allowing the bird to spread them and flap them up and down.

Birds are much lighter than other animals of the same size. Their bones are partly hollow with a honeycomb structure inside. The framework provides strength, while the air pockets keep the bones light. Feathers provide a warm outer covering without adding much weight. Each feather has a long, narrow shaft running down the center. Hundreds of thin branches called barbs *stick out on each side. The barbs in turn have tinier branches, each with little hooks that hold together like Velcro. A bird spends a lot of time preening its feathers: It cleans them with its* bill *(beak), spreads oil from special skin glands over them, and smooths out the barbs so that they fit together and form a light but solid surface.*

The main flight feathers, called primaries, *are located at the tips of the wings and can be spread out like fingers. They help the bird to rise into the air, steer, and soar across the sky. The feathers closer to the body are called* secondaries *and help to keep the bird warm.*

A bird's two legs may be used for walking on the ground and for climbing and perching on tree branches. Most birds' feet have four toes, which end in sharp claws used for grasping things. Waterbirds, such as ducks, have webs of skin between their toes that help in swimming.

A bird's jaws have a tough, horny covering and form a bill, or beak. Birds don't have teeth to chew their food. They either cut it up with their bill into bite-size chunks or gobble it up whole. Food is stored temporarily in a baglike pouch in the neck, called the crop, *then digested when the bird gets back to the safety of its roost.*

WHAT A PET!

THIS SERIES WILL GIVE you information about some well-known animals and some unusual ones. It will help you to select a pet suitable for your family and for where you live. It will also tell you about animals that should not be pets. It is important for you to understand that many people who work with animals are strongly opposed to keeping any wild creature as a pet.

People tend to want to keep exotic animals. But they forget that often it is illegal to have them as pets, or that they require a great deal of special care and will never really become good pets. A current fad of owning an exotic animal may quickly pass, and the animals suffer. Their owners may abandon them in an effort to return them to the wild, even though the animals can no longer survive there. Or they may languish in small cages without proper food and exercise.

Before selecting any animal as a pet, it is a good idea to learn as much as you can about it. This series will help you, and your local veterinarian and the American Society for the Prevention of Cruelty to Animals (ASPCA) are good sources of information. You should also find out if it is endangered. Phone numbers for each state wildlife agency can be found on the Internet at

www.rzu2u.com/states.htm

Any pet is a big responsibility—your responsibility. The most important thing to keep in mind when selecting a pet is the welfare of the animal.

FAST FACTS

Scientific name	*Psittacus erithacus* in Family Psittacida
Cost	$900 to $1,300
Food	Pellet food (sold in pet stores); diet should also include seeds, fruits (such as apples, grapes, bananas), and vegeta bles (such as broccoli, carrots, celery, corn). Calcium is very important in the diet. Cuttlebone (sold in pet shops) is a good source of calcium. They can also get it from calcium-rich foods, includin broccoli, kale, apricots, cabbage, bean lemons, limes, oranges, eggs, almonds and hazelnuts.
Housing	Cage at least 30 inches (75 cm) square Should include a variety of perches of different sizes and textures, a water bottle, and plenty of toys to keep the bird occupied. A cover (a sheet or towel) should be placed over the cage at night. This will keep the bird calm, eliminate drafts, and act as a signal tha it's bedtime.
Training	They can be taught to speak words or make sounds like whistles or a tele-phone's ring. They can also be trained perch on the owner's hand or arm.
Special Notes	African grays have powder in their down feathers, which can aggravate allergies in people.

AFRICAN GRAY PARROT

"POLLY WANT A CRACKER?" Pirates who sailed the seas long ago said that to the pet parrots they kept for company during their voyages. Most parrots can mimic, or copy, sounds that they hear. African grays are said to be the best talkers of all the parrots. They not only can talk, they actually understand what they are saying.

Owning a talking parrot sounds like a lot of fun. But African grays are very shy, and it can take a lot of patience to tame them. And they may not necessarily talk when you want them to!

AFRICAN GRAYS IN THE WILD

African gray parrots are found in much of Central Africa, from the Guinea islands in the western region over to northwest Tanzania and Kenya. These birds, sometimes called Congo African grays, do not have the bright colors seen in most other parrots. Instead, they are gray with a solid black beak and a bright red tail. Their body measures 12 to 14 inches (30 to 35 cm) long.

The Timneh African gray is also native to Central Africa, although its range is more limited. This bird is smaller, about 10 inches (25 cm) long, and darker, with a maroon-colored tail. The Timneh's upper beak is reddish gray to pink, unlike the black beak of the "typical" African gray.

In the wild, African grays are commonly found in lowland forests, roosting in tall trees that overlook the water. They live together in large groups, called *flocks*. The flocks roost together, chattering away, and fly together in search of food. Wild African grays feed on flowers, leaves, nuts, seeds, fruits, and berries. They cause so much damage to maize (corn) crops that local farmers consider them pests. These parrots are extremely shy and very sensitive to danger. If humans come too close, they will quickly fly away.

During the breeding season, mating pairs leave the flock and nest together in a deep hole in a tree that is high above the ground. Usually only one pair occupies a tree. The female lays three to five eggs over a few days. She sits on them for about thirty days, while the male feeds her and protects the nest.

DID YOU KNOW?
Parrots belong to the family Psittacidae, which means to repeat something. That's because parrots are known for repeating sounds they hear.

After the chicks hatch, the parents feed and care for them and teach them the skills they need to survive. The parents continue to care for their young for some time even after they grow their flight feathers and learn how to fly.

What Is a Parrot?

The name parrot describes a large group of colorful birds that lives mainly in the tropical regions of Africa, Asia, Australia, and South and Central America. There are more than three hundred species of parrots. They vary greatly, from only 3 inches (8 cm) to more than 3 feet (90 cm) long. Some popular parrots are macaws, parakeets, Amazons, conures, cockatoos and cockatiels, lories and lorikeets, budgerigars, lovebirds, and, of course, African gray parrots.

Most parrots share two distinct traits. They have a powerful, hooked beak, good for cracking open fruit and nuts. They also have unusual feet, in which two toes point forward and the other two point backward. Their strong feet help them to grip firmly onto branches as well as to hold onto food and objects.

AFRICAN GRAYS AS PETS

African grays are not domesticated animals. Cats and dogs are separated from their wild ancestors by thousands of generations, but pet parrots are only one or two generations removed from the wild. So their wild instincts are still very strong.

Young African grays can become tame if they are given plenty of love and attention. (Adults are difficult if not impossible to tame.) They can form close bonds with their owners. However, all family members should spend a lot of time with the bird; otherwise, it will become attached to just one person—the one who feeds it, cleans the cage, and plays with it. African grays are especially shy around strangers and may become quiet and withdrawn. These birds are very sensitive and should never be scolded during training. They respond best to praise and treats.

With such high intelligence, African grays can get bored easily, especially during the day when their owners are away at school or at work. These parrots may pluck out their own feathers when they get bored or frustrated. Make sure that they have plenty of toys to keep them busy.

African grays love to spend time with their family. A portable perch allows you to move your bird to wherever the action is. But keep the bird in its cage when nobody is home. If left to roam freely without supervision, it may injure itself or cause damage. An intelligent, curious bird could get into dangerous things such as poisonous houseplants or electrical cords. It might also rip apart furniture and other household items with its strong beak.

LOOK WHO'S TALKING

Some experts consider African grays the best talkers among parrots, but many don't talk until they are one to two years old—and some hardly talk at all. The best time to teach parrots to speak is when they are young. It is very important for the bird to develop a good relationship with its owner first. A bird that feels comfortable and secure is more likely to speak.

Parrots don't have vocal cords like ours. They make sounds by forcing air across the top of the trachea (breathing tube), much like blowing over the top of a soda bottle. The bird can make different sounds by changing the shape of its trachea. This takes a lot of practice before it can make sounds we can understand. A parrot starts off babbling and muttering, much like a human baby. As it continues to practice making sounds, words and phrases should be repeated to the bird often. Soon it will pick up words and eventually will be able to speak in phrases and sentences. What's more, the bird will understand the meaning of the words and can tell you when it's hungry, afraid, or bored.

African grays can sound just like the person they are imitating. They can also make a variety of familiar sounds—whistling, telephones, doorbells, sirens, microwave ovens, chainsaws, and a barking dog.

One Smart Bird

An African gray named Prudle is listed in the Guinness Book of World Records *as the best talking bird, with a vocabulary of nearly 1,000 words. But the smartest bird is an African gray named Alex. Biologist Irene Pepperberg began a study on communicating with birds back in 1977. Alex, born in 1976, was her pet project. While Alex doesn't know nearly as many words as Prudle, he has learned to count to six, identify objects, shapes, colors, and materials, and knows the concepts of same and different. Dr. Pepperberg and her assistants are now working with phonics and hope that Alex will someday learn to read.*

African grays are truly remarkable birds, and keeping them can be a unique experience. But they are a huge responsibility and a lifelong commitment. These birds can live up to fifty years!

INTERNET RESOURCES

www.itsagreysworld.com/articles/faq.htm "FAQ—It's a Grey's World"

www.minorkey.com/greys.html "The Pet African Grey Parrot"

www.parrot.thepampurredpet.com/bungalow/african-grey-parrot.php3
     "African Grey Parrot"

www.upatsix.com/faq/greyfaq.htm "The Grey Parrot FAQ" by Mike and Beth Holland

FAST FACTS

Scientific name	*Melopsittacus undulatus* in Family Psittacidae
Cost	$10 to $20
Food	Parrot seed or pellet food (sold in pet stores); diet should also include fruits (such as apples, pears, cantaloupe), and vegetables (such as broccoli, carrots, corn, green beans, peas). Cuttle-bone is also good for nibbling and provides calcium as well.
Housing	Cage at least 18 inches (46 cm) square. Should include perches of different sizes and textures, twigs (for nibbling), a water bottle, and plenty of toys (ladders, swings, mirrors) to keep the bird occupied. A cover (a sheet or towel) should be placed over the cage at night. This will keep the bird calm, eliminate drafts, and act as a signal that it's bedtime.
Training	They can be taught to speak words or make whistling sounds. Can be trained to perch on your finger.
Special Notes	Budgies need exercise. They should be allowed to fly freely only in bird-proof rooms with no dangerous objects, open windows or doors, and no roaming cats, dogs, or other predators. They should always be supervised. Some experts say that the wings should be clipped regularly to keep the birds from flying into trouble.

BUDGERIGAR

WALK INTO ALMOST ANY PET store and chances are you will see some colorful little birds called budgerigars, or budgies for short. Budgies are among the most popular pet birds in the entire world. These birds are actually small parrots. They are quieter than other parrots and can learn how to talk, too.

Budgies are a good choice for people who would like to keep a parrot but don't have enough room for a large one. These friendly little birds are easy to tame and can learn to perch happily on your finger.

A BUDGIE'S LIFE

Budgies are native to much of Australia. They live in hot, dry regions, usually in open country scattered with trees and bushes. With very little rainfall, budgies have to move from place to place in search of food and water. They travel in enormous flocks that number in the thousands and look like a huge dark cloud moving across the sky.

Staying in a flock helps to protect budgies from predators. Whether traveling, sleeping, or eating, the birds stay together. When some members of the flock are threatened, all of them fly away together and look for a new place to roost.

When the flock reaches a new destination, the hungry little birds search the ground for grass seeds and tiny insects and drink whatever water is available. Then they rest in the holes of nearby eucalyptus trees. Their green-and-yellow color helps budgies hide from predators, but many of these little birds are eaten. Hawks and falcons snatch them in midair with their strong talons (claws), and snakes gobble up young budgies in their nest.

During very long dry periods, budgies may have to fly hundreds of miles to find enough food and water. When these conditions go on for too long, many do not survive. To make up for their losses,

> **DID YOU KNOW?**
> Budgies are commonly called parakeets in the United States. But bird experts use the name parakeet to describe certain small parrot-type birds with long tails. Basically, budgies are parakeets, but not all parakeets are budgies.

> **DID YOU KNOW?**
> Budgies are fast fliers. They can travel more than 70 miles (113 km) per hour.

budgies are great breeders. They are ready to breed when they are just a few months old. When a budgie finds a mate, it has a partner for life. Breeding usually starts after a rainfall, when there is enough food and water for young budgies. The mated pair finds a nesting site, usually in a tree hollow, or in rotting wood, under rocks, or in holes in the ground. Often several pairs nest in a single tree.

The female budgie lays four to six eggs. While she sits on the eggs, the male brings food back to his mate and keeps her company. When the chicks hatch more than two weeks later, the male continues to bring back food, and both parents feed the chicks. By five to six weeks, the young budgies have grown their flight feathers and are ready to leave the nest. Even after they learn how to fly, their parents continue to feed them until they learn to find food on their own. As soon as the young budgies are able to live independently, the mother is ready to breed again.

THE FIRST PET BUDGIES

The name *budgerigar* comes from an Australian Aboriginal word meaning "good food," which shows how the natives used budgies. These birds were first noted by English settlers in the late 1700s. In 1840 a visiting English naturalist, John Gould, was intrigued by the colorful little birds. When he returned to England, he brought along some young budgies that had been taken from a wild nest and hand-reared by his brother-in-law, Charles Coxon. People were fascinated by these adorable little birds. The first pair was sold for £27. (In today's money, that would be more than $1,000.)

At first, budgies were very expensive and sold mostly to the wealthy. Sailors, hoping to make some extra money, started to trap large numbers of wild budgies to take back to England. But many of the birds died on the long journey, and soon the wild budgie population was dwindling.

Fortunately, the birds that did survive were easy to breed in captivity. By the late 1850s, English breeders began to offer captive-bred budgies for sale. As more became available, their cost dropped rapidly; in fact, an advertisement in *Field* magazine in 1859 quoted a price of only £2 for a pair. Soon almost anybody could buy these birds, and they quickly spread throughout Europe and then to America and other parts of the world.

In 1894, Australia made it illegal to catch and trade wild budgies. Eventually, the wild population recovered. Meanwhile, captive breeding continued to expand. By the early 1900s budgies were being bred by the hundreds of thousands. (Today, all budgies sold in pet shops are bred in captivity.) Breeders created many new color variations, including the popular blue colorations, which are not seen in the wild. Blue budgies probably would not survive long in the wild because this color does not make good camouflage like the usual yellow and green.

BUDGIES AS PETS

There are two kinds of budgies: the American budgie and the English budgie. The American budgie is commonly sold in pet stores. It is about 7 inches (18 cm) long and can live up to fifteen years (a few have lived as long as thirty years). The English budgie is bred for show. It is bigger and stockier, about 10 inches (25 cm) long, with a larger head and chest. It also has a shorter life span—five to seven years. American budgies may live for only a few years if not cared for properly. Budgies are friendly creatures and easy to tame. Teaching the bird to perch on your finger is a great way to bond with your pet. Since budgies are very social by nature, they need lots of attention. Unless you can devote all your time to your pet, you should keep at least two birds. Two males or one male and one female make the best pairs. (Two females tend to squabble a lot.) A male and female will not mate if there is no nesting box.

Budgies can learn to say words and phrases. Some have been known to learn as many as a hundred words. But budgies cannot mimic their owner's voice, like an African gray, or speak as clearly and loudly. Some budgies sold in pet shops are adults, which are too old to start learning to speak. How do you know if you have a young budgie? Young budgies have colored bars running across the forehead. These bars disappear around three months of age. They should be taught to speak before this age.

Male or Female?

Males are usually better talkers than females. So how can you tell your budgie's sex? The key is the cere, *a waxy area at the top of the beak surrounding the nostrils. The cere of an adult male is blue or purplish, while an adult female's is white or beige.*

INTERNET RESOURCES

ca.essortment.com/budgiesparakeet_pbc.htm "Budgies (parakeets) as pets!"

www.budgies.org/info/faq.html "Me & My Budgie—Budgie FAQ"

www.petplace.com/Articles/artShow.asp?artID=2978 "Choosing a Budgie or Parakeet"

www.sspca.net/budgie.htm "Budgerigars"

FAST FACTS

Scientific name	*Cacatua galerita* (greater sulphur-crested cockatoo), *Cacatua sulphurea* (lesser sulphur-crested cockatoo), *Cacatua molluccensis* (Mollucan cockatoo) in Family Psittacidae
Cost	$400 to $1,000 for most; some species may cost $1,500 to $3,000 or more.
Food	Pellet food (sold in pet stores); diet should also include seeds, fruits (such as apples, pears, cantaloupe), and vegetables (such as broccoli, carrots, corn, green beans, peas). Cuttlebone is also good for nibbling and provides calcium as well.
Housing	Steel or metal cage (not wood!) at least 27 by 27 by 39 inches (70 x 70 x 100 cm), with a padlock. Should include perches of different sizes and textures, twigs (for nibbling), a water bottle, and plenty of toys (chains with large links, climbing ropes, fresh branches for gnawing) to keep the bird occupied. A cover (a sheet or towel) should be placed over the cage at night. This will keep the bird calm, eliminate drafts, and act as a signal that it's bedtime.
Training	Can be taught to speak a few words and make whistling sounds. Can be trained to perch on your arm. If you let them perch on your shoulder, they may become too dominant.
Special Notes	Cockatoos need exercise. They need to be carefully supervised if allowed to fly freely in the home. They are such powerful fliers that their wings should be clipped to keep them from crashing into walls and windows. These birds will pluck their breast feathers if bored, so provide plenty of toys to keep them busy during the day.

COCKATOO

HAVE YOU EVER SEEN a parrot ride a little bicycle, use roller skates, or walk a tightrope? Cockatoos are often the stars of bird shows because they can do such tricks and more. These birds are very clever and can accomplish amazing feats, but they aren't the best talkers. In fact, many of them can say just a few words, while others can only make sounds.

Cockatoos can form strong bonds with their owners. However, this bird is not a good choice for everyone. Cockatoos make loud, screeching calls. Many people have difficulty living with them.

A COCKATOO'S LIFE

Cockatoos come from Australia, Indonesia, and nearby islands. Some species live in the plains and desert regions, while others are found in tropical rain forests. Like other parrots, cockatoos live in flocks. In the dry, desert areas, thousands of birds in a single flock can be seen searching for food, although flocks of forty to fifty birds are more common. In the tropical rain forests, flocks contain far fewer birds, averaging about eight to ten.

Cockatoos are excellent fliers and will travel far in search of food. (They make loud calls along the way, which can be deafening in very large groups.) The flock gathers together at the same food site. A cockatoo has a strong, hooked beak that can crack open seeds, nuts, fruits, and vegetables. The bird uses its feet like hands, holding onto a piece of food and bringing it to its beak.

All cockatoos have feathered crests on their heads. In some species, the crest is very long and showy, while in others it is rather short. The crest is used to show the bird's mood. If it is excited or frightened, it may raise its crest feathers. The crest also plays an important part in the mating ritual. When a male wants to impress a female, he puts on a display for her. Spreading his wings and tail, he ruffles his feathers and raises his crest. He then struts around, bobbing his head up and down, then side to side. The male's display also acts as a warning sign to other males to stay away or else! Male cockatoos will fight over a female during the breeding season.

DID YOU KNOW?
Cockatoos are best known for the large feathered crests on top of their heads.

DID YOU KNOW?
The cockatoo's beak is a multi-purpose tool. It is used like a can opener, for climbing, and to widen a nesting site.

If the female likes what she sees, the mating pair will leave the flock and search for a good nesting site. Like other parrots, cockatoos nest in tree hollows, usually near a water source. The two birds form a close bond during their courtship. They spend a lot of time scratching and preening each other. Soon the female lays two to five white eggs, which take twenty-eight to thirty days to hatch. The male and female take turns sitting on the eggs and feeding the young. The young cockatoos are ready to leave the nest after six to eight weeks.

What Do Baby Birds Eat?

In the first days of life, newborn chicks need to eat soft, mashed food. When their parents go off to search for food, they eat it first. Then they come back to the nest and regurgitate (spit up) the partly digested food into their chicks' open mouths. As they get older, the young birds will be able to handle solid food, which their parents bring to them.

COCKATOOS AS PETS

The cockatoos most commonly kept as pets are the greater sulphur-crested cockatoo, the lesser sulphur-crested cockatoo, and the Moluccan cockatoo. Cockatoos are not brightly colored like other parrots. Most are white, but some species come in black or pink, and their crest and tail may be colored differently. The greater sulphur-crested cockatoo is probably the best-known cockatoo. This parrot, which grows to about 20 inches (50 cm) long, is white with a bright yellow crest and yellow underneath the wings and tail feathers. The lesser looks very similar to the greater, but it is smaller, growing to about 13 inches (32 cm) long.

A Better Pet

Cockatiels look like smaller versions of cockatoos. In fact, they were called cockatoo parrots at first because they, too, had feathered crests. The name was later changed when people realized that this was a different kind of bird.

Cockatiels are usually gray with white patches on the wings. They were found in Australia in 1840, around the same time budgies were discovered. Like budgies, cockatiels became good breeders in captivity. These birds are quiet and gentle and soon were a favorite in bird keeping. Actually, cockatiels make much better pets than cockatoos. They are not loud screechers, and they are fairly easy to care for.

Cockatoos love attention and enjoy being included in family activities. They can become friendly and lovable, especially if you start with a young bird. Cockatoos are very sociable and should not be left alone for long periods of time. They will make loud, screeching calls when they are bored or lonely. This can be a problem, especially if you live in an apartment. You may get a lot of complaints from neighbors. Cockatoos cannot be trained not to screech since they are noisy birds by nature.

Cockatoos are very intelligent. They can undo latches and escape from their cage; you'll need a padlock to keep them in. If they are allowed to roam freely unsupervised, they can get into trouble. They may injure themselves, escape through an open door or window, or do a lot of damage to furniture, houseplants, and other items with their strong, sharp beaks. It is best to get the largest cage you can afford for these big birds. Cages should be made of metal, not wood, which cockatoos will just chew up.

Cockatoos are famous for their amazing ability to learn tricks. They can be taught to play tug-of-war, carry objects around, push little toy cars, dance to music, or even whistle tunes and use one of their feet to "conduct." Training takes a lot of patience. It is important to give your pet plenty of praise for a job well done, and don't forget the treats.

Cockatoos are a big responsibility. They have special needs, require a large amount of space, and are very expensive compared to smaller parrots, such as budgies. Make sure you do plenty of research on cockatoos so that you know what you're getting into. This is a long-term commitment since cockatoos can live forty to sixty years or more!

INTERNET RESOURCES

www.cockatoos.org/ "1 Stop For Parrot & Cockatoo Information"

www.geocities.com/RainForest/Vines/1492/cockatoos.html "Cockatoos!!"

www.parrot-haven-aviary.com.au/Sulphur-crested.htm "Parrot Haven Aviary"

FAST FACTS

Scientific name	*Agapornis roseicollis* (peach-faced lovebird); *Agapornis personata fischeri* (Fischer's lovebird); *Agapornis personata personata* (masked lovebird); in Family Psittacidae
Cost	$25 to $200
Food	Pellet food (sold in pet stores); diet should also include seeds, fruits (such as apples, pears, cantaloupe), and vegetables (such as broccoli, carrots, corn, green beans, peas). Cuttlebone is good for nibbling and provides calcium as well.
Housing	Cage at least 18 inches (46 cm) square. Should include perches of different sizes and textures, twigs (for nibbling), a water bottle, and plenty of toys (ladders, swings, climbing chains, mirrors) to keep the bird occupied. A cover (a sheet or towel) should be placed over the cage at night. This will keep the bird calm, eliminate drafts, and act as a signal that it's bedtime.
Training	They can be taught to make whistling sounds. Can be trained to perch on your finger.
Special Notes	Lovebirds need exercise. They should be allowed to fly freely only in bird-proof rooms with no dangerous objects, open windows or doors, or roaming cats, dogs, or other predators. They should always be supervised. Some experts say the birds' wings should be clipped regularly to keep them from flying into trouble.

LOVEBIRD

YOU CAN LEARN ABOUT LOVE by watching a couple of lovebirds. These colorful little parrots spend a lot of time sitting together in pairs, grooming each other, feeding each other, and traveling together. This constant display of affection is what gave them their name.

Lovebirds are not talking parrots. They do like to chatter a lot, and can be a little noisy at times, but they are not nearly as loud as cockatoos.

LOVEBIRDS IN THE WILD

Lovebirds are small parrots with short, round tails. They can be found in Africa, Madagascar, and nearby islands. There are only nine species, but their habitats vary greatly. Some species live in the mountains, in elevations as high as 10,000 feet (3,000 m) above sea level. Others can be found in open fields, forests, plains, and even swamps.

Lovebirds form close-knit pairs at a very young age, usually after their first molt (shedding of old, worn feathers). These pairs become partners for life. They do everything together, whether it's sitting, grooming, searching for food, or escaping from enemies. Lovebirds usually travel in small flocks of about ten to twenty pairs. Together they feed on grass seeds, grains, berries, and fruit. They can do a lot of damage to crops, and therefore can be quite a problem for farmers.

> **DID YOU KNOW?**
> Many people believe that a lovebird will die of loneliness without its mate. This is not true.

At breeding time, they come together in larger colonies, and several pairs can be found at a single nesting site. Lovebirds are very territorial, though, and despite their loving nature toward their mates, they will viciously attack any other birds that get too close.

Lovebirds usually nest in tree hollows, but some may nest in termite mounds or anything else that is handy. The nesting site is usually near a water source because they like to drink a lot of water. Unlike most parrots, the female lovebird actually builds a nest using various materials, possibly including twigs, leaves, grasses, and moss. Most lovebirds carry things in their beaks, but some tuck the nesting materials between their body feathers, especially around the back and rump. The female lays her eggs every other day. She may lay as many as eight eggs, but four to six is the average. While the female sits on the eggs, the male feeds her. He also sleeps next to her to keep her company in the nest. It will take about twenty-one to twenty-four days for each egg to hatch. The chicks get their flight feathers in about thirty-eight to forty-five days. The parents continue to feed their young even after they leave the nest.

It's Molting Time

All birds have to molt, and lovebirds are no exception. Before baby lovebirds can leave the nest, they lose some of their down feathers as the adult feathers grow in. The first "real" molt takes place about three or four months later. Then every year thereafter, the adult bird molts again, around the end of the breeding season. The old, worn-out feathers are replaced with new ones. Fortunately, this doesn't happen all at once. A few feathers fall out and are soon replaced by new ones. This process continues again and again until all of the feathers have been replaced. The lovebird is never bald during the whole molting process, and it never loses so many flight feathers that it cannot fly.

LOVEBIRDS AS PETS

Three kinds of lovebirds are commonly sold as pets: the peach-faced lovebird, the Fischer's lovebird, and the masked lovebird. These colorful parrots are 5 to 7 inches (13 to 18 cm) long and can live for more than ten years. The peach-faced lovebird is the most popular pet choice. It has a peach-colored face (sometimes described as pinkish red), green wings and body, and a cobalt-blue color on its tail and rump feathers.

Lovebirds do not have to be kept in pairs. Actually, you have a better chance of bonding with your bird if you have only one. However, lovebirds are very social and need lots of attention. If the bird is left alone for long periods of time, it will be very unhappy. In that case, you should probably keep a pair to keep them from getting lonely. Lovebirds do not always live up to their sweet reputation, though. If you put two birds together and they are not compatible, one may attack the other viciously. In the wild, lovebirds pick their own mates.

In many species, male and female birds have different colored feathers. But for the peach-faced lovebird, as well as most other lovebird species, the male and female look similar and it is not easy tell the difference. You can usually find out whether you have a male and female pair when it's time to breed. (Males don't lay eggs.) Tests can also be done, but they can be expensive. Pet shops often do not bother, so you may find that the "pair" you bought are both of the same sex. It is best to get a "true pair" from a breeder who specializes in lovebirds.

What's Inside?

You can find out if an egg is fertile (capable of developing into a growing chick) by holding it up to a light. If the egg is fertile, you will see a black spot surrounded by blood vessels. If it isn't, the egg appears clear and eventually turns yellow. If your lovebird is laying infertile eggs, you may have two females. Or the birds may not be in top physical condition, so you may need to change their diet or housing conditions.

Lovebirds can be tamed, although not as easily as budgies. It is best to start with a very young bird or one that is hand-raised. The more time you spend with your pet, the friendlier it will become. Soon it will learn to perch on your finger, wander through your hair, or even snuggle in your shirt pocket. Lovebirds can form strong bonds with their owners. However, they tend to be one-person birds. And even though the bird may be affectionate toward its owner, it will not feel the same way about other members of the family. If anybody else tries to pick it up or even feed it, the bird may attack the person, pecking at his or her hand.

Lovebirds are very active and love to climb and hang upside down on their toys. They need exercise outside the cage, as well. But they should be carefully watched so they don't get hurt.

Lovebirds like to chatter a lot and make chirping sounds. Sometimes they can be rather noisy and will make high-pitched shrieking sounds. But they are not nearly as noisy as their larger parrot relatives. Find out more about lovebirds to see if they are the right birds for you.

INTERNET RESOURCES

www.birdsnways.com/articles/lbfaq.htm "Lovebird FAQ" by Nicole Jones

www.birdsnways.com/wisdom/ww49eiii.htm "What You Need To Know About Keeping Lovebirds"

www.birdtimes.com/breeds/lovebird.shtml "Lovebirds" by John C. Tyson

FAST FACTS

Scientific name	*Ara ararauna* (blue-and-gold macaw), *Ara macao* (scarlet macaw) in Family Psittacidae
Cost	$900 to $1,400 for blue-and-gold macaw; a scarlet macaw costs $1,200 to $1,600.
Food	Pellet food (sold in pet stores); diet should also include seeds, fruits (such as apples, pears, cantaloupe), and vegetables (such as broccoli, carrots, corn, green beans, peas). Cuttlebone is good for nibbling and provides calcium as well. Pet macaws do not need to eat clay because their food does not contain toxins.
Housing	Steel or metal cage (not wood!) at least 30 by 36 by 65 inches (76 x 91 x 165 cm), with a padlock. Should include perches of different sizes and textures, twigs or wood pieces (for nibbling), a water bottle, and plenty of toys (chains with large links, climbing ropes, fresh branches for gnawing) to keep the bird occupied. A cover (a sheet or towel) should be placed over the cage at night. This will keep the bird calm, eliminate drafts, and act as a signal that it's bedtime.
Training	Can be taught to speak a few words and make whistling sounds. Can be trained to perch on your arm. If you let them perch on your shoulder, they may become too dominant.
Special Notes	Macaws need exercise. They should be allowed to fly freely only in bird-proof rooms with no dangerous objects, open windows or doors, and roaming cats, dogs, or other predators. They should always be supervised. Some experts say the birds' wings should be clipped regularly to keep them from flying into trouble.

MACAW

WHEN YOU THINK OF A PARROT, you are probably picturing a macaw. Its large size and colorful feathers make it the most recognizable of all the parrots. While the macaw may look like a "typical" parrot, though, it's not a very good talker.

Macaws are strikingly beautiful birds, but they are not a good choice for inexperienced bird keepers. These birds make very loud, screeching calls, which can be very difficult to live with.

Pirate's Pet

In the famous adventure story Treasure Island, *the pirate Long John Silver had a pet parrot that perched on his shoulder. Although Long John was a fictional character, real-life pirates often kept pet parrots that they had bought in tropical ports. Pictures of pirates usually show them with macaws.*

MACAWS IN THE WILD

Macaws are the largest of all parrots. They can grow up to 39 inches (99 cm) long, half of which is their long tail. Some macaws, though, are much smaller, measuring only 12 inches (30 cm) long.

Macaws live mostly in the tropical rain forests of Mexico, Central and South America, and nearby islands. They can be found in river valleys, swamps, grasslands, and the mountains. Rain forests are tropical forests in which evergreen trees grow very closely together. A lot of rain falls in the rain forest, usually at least 100 inches (254 cm) per year. The trees in a rain forest are very tall, many growing to more than 100 feet (30 m) high.

The broad leaves and branches high up on the trees form a covering over the forest, called a canopy. Macaws spend a lot of time in the canopy resting and searching for food. The canopy also helps to protect them from predators, such as cats and reptiles, that live down on the ground. However, they may be killed by predators that can fly, such as harpy eagles.

Macaws live in small flocks, usually up to twenty birds, but there may be more than a hundred of them, sitting together at their roosting sites. In such large groups their loud screeches are deafening. During the day, the macaws search for food and will fly long distances to find something good to eat. They feed mostly on seeds, but they will also eat nuts, berries, and leaves.

Macaws are very skillful birds. They can hang upside down from a branch by one foot and grab a piece of fruit with the other. Like many other parrots, a macaw uses one of its feet like a hand to feed itself. Its large, powerful beak works like a third "foot" in climbing from one branch to another. The beak is also used to crack open fruit and nuts so that the macaw can gather up the tasty contents with its tongue.

In the rain forest, many seeds contain toxins (poisons) that are harmful to most animals. But macaws don't get sick when they eat these poisonous seeds. That's because macaws spend a lot of time at riverbanks eating clay, which traps the poisons and helps to move them through the body quickly. So the poisons don't stay in the bird's body very long. If wild macaws didn't eat clay, they would get very sick.

Macaws are very slow to mature. It may take five years until they are ready to breed. During the breeding season, pairs leave the flock and look for a nesting site. Macaws usually nest in the holes of dead trees, high above the ground. Some nest in the cavities of cliff faces. The mating pair spends some time getting to know one another by cleaning each other's feathers, touching each other's beaks, and flying close together so that their wings almost touch.

The female may lay up to four eggs, although two to three is the average. She sits on the eggs for twenty-four to twenty-eight days. In the meantime, the male is busy looking for food and bringing it back to feed his mate. He is also on guard duty, protecting the nest from any intruders. When the eggs hatch, both parents take turns feeding the baby chicks until they have their flight feathers and are ready to leave the nest. That may take as long as three months. The parents continue to take care of their young and teach them even after they become independent, for up to two years.

MACAWS AS PETS

There are seventeen species of macaws, but the blue-and-gold macaw is the most popular. This bird, which measures up to 36 inches (91 cm) long, is brightly colored with a green crown, blue on the back and tail feathers, and yellow on the underside. Around the eyes are several rows of black feathers on its bare, white face. The blue-and-gold macaw breeds very well in captivity and is widely available. Another popular macaw is the scarlet macaw (also called the red-and-gold macaw). It is slightly smaller than the blue-and-gold macaw, measuring up to 34 inches (86 cm). The scarlet macaw is mostly a deep red color, with yellow and green markings on blue wings.

When macaws are hand-raised from a young age, they can form close bonds with their human family. Some macaws are one-person birds, but blue-and-gold macaws tend to get along well with all family members.

Macaws are not as good talkers as African grays. But they are very smart and can learn to do tricks, such as riding a little bicycle, rolling over, and lying on their back and playing dead. They can also do acrobatic stunts. They like to swing on a rope, climb upside down across the roof of their cage, and even hang from their cage by only their beak.

Keeping macaws is a huge responsibility and not a good choice for beginners. Because of their large size, macaws need a very large cage and lots of room to move around. This can be very expensive. These birds are also very noisy. They make loud shrieks, screams, and calls—and there's no way to stop them. This can make a macaw owner unpopular with the neighbors!

Macaws love to chew things. If they are left alone and don't have enough toys to keep from getting bored, they can do a great deal of damage to furniture and other household items. These birds should be watched carefully if they are allowed to roam inside the home. Cages must be sturdy with a strong padlock because they can learn to undo latches.

Owning a macaw is a big decision that you will have to live with for a very long time. Macaws can live up to seventy years!

INTERNET RESOURCES

gecko.gc.maricopa.edu/~bjlombar/Project/Blugld.html "Blue and Gold Macaws"

www.geocities.com/Petsburgh/3095/macaws.html "Information about Blue and Gold Macaws"

www.harrisonsbirdfoods.com/brochure/macaws.html "The Companion Bird Care Series: Macaws"

FAST FACTS

Scientific name	*Serinus canaria* (canary) in Family Fringillidae, subfamily Carduelinae
Cost	$10 to $125, depending on type of canary
Food	Canary seed (sold in pet stores); diet should also include spinach, celery, peas, watercress, apples, bananas, dandelions, lettuce (not iceberg, which has fewer nutrients), and oranges. Cuttlebone is a good source of calcium.
Housing	A rectangular cage at least 20 inches (51 cm) long for a pair. Should include perches of different sizes and textures, a water bottle, and only one or two playthings (a toy, a branch, or a swing). Canaries should be able to fly from one perch to another with few things in the way. A cover (a sheet or towel) should be placed over the cage at night. This will keep the bird calm, eliminate drafts, and act as a signal that it's bedtime.
Training	Can be taught to imitate some song selections. Can be trained to perch on your finger or arm.
Special Notes	Canaries need exercise. They should be allowed to fly freely only in bird-proof rooms with no dangerous objects, open windows or doors, and roaming cats, dogs, or other predators. They should always be supervised. Some experts say the birds' wings should be clipped regularly to keep them from flying into trouble. Keep cage on a stand at least 6 feet (1.8 m) off the floor or hang it from a bracket on the wall or ceiling. In the wild, canaries are attacked from above, by predatory birds.

CANARY

CANARIES MAY NOT BE ABLE TO TALK like some parrots, but oh, how they can sing! These little songbirds use their sweet-sounding voices to communicate with other members of their species.

Their beautiful songs have made canaries popular pets for hundreds of years. But if you want a singing canary, you may not get what you want. Not all canaries are great singers.

CANARIES IN THE WILD

Canaries were named after the Canary Islands, a group of Spanish islands in the Atlantic Ocean off the coast of northwestern Africa. Wild canaries are still found on the Canary Islands, in a variety of habitats, from forests to open country. They live wherever there are trees and bushes for roosting and nesting.

Wild canaries look different from their domesticated relatives. These little greenish-brown birds are not easy to spot, as they stay hidden among the trees and bushes. But you can hear them singing even if you can't see them.

> **DID YOU KNOW?**
> Singing comes naturally to canaries, but these little songbirds can be taught to improve their singing voices.

Canaries live together in flocks of fifty or more birds. They fly long distances across the islands in search of tasty grass seeds and weeds. During the breeding season, from winter to spring, male canaries become very territorial. They like to nest with their mates in an isolated tree or bush, usually no more than 10 feet (3 m) from the ground. The male sings a special song, which gets louder and more constant during the breeding season. This song lets the female know that he is ready to mate, but it also warns other males to stay away! If another male tries to invade the singing male's territory, a fight may break out.

If the female likes the male's serenade, she will make a small, cup-shaped nest from grasses, thin stems and twigs, leaves, and moss. Then she lines the nest with feathers and other soft materials. Soon after mating, the female lays three to five pale blue eggs. Once all the eggs are laid, she sits on them, keeping them warm. The male's job is to feed his mate so she can stay with the eggs as much as possible. They do not take turns sitting on the eggs.

27

After thirteen to fourteen days, all the eggs hatch at the same time. The male continues to feed the female and brings back food for the baby chicks, too. The young chicks grow very quickly. About fifteen days later, they have all their flight feathers and are getting ready to leave the nest. The parents continue to feed their young for about ten more days. The father teaches the young chicks how to find food on their own. Meanwhile, the female gets ready to lay another batch of eggs. After the breeding season, the bird families come together in flocks.

THE DOMESTICATED CANARY

Spanish soldiers were fascinated by the singing canaries they saw when they conquered the Canary Islands more than five hundred years ago. Between 1478 and 1496, the Spaniards took large numbers of wild canaries back home with them. Many of these cute little songbirds were given to people as gifts and soon earned a sweet reputation. As their popularity grew, the price for canaries soared, and only the wealthy could afford them.

It didn't take long for sailors to realize that they could make a lot of money selling canaries. Large numbers were captured and brought back to Spain. Unfortunately, many little birds did not survive the long, difficult voyage back home.

Meanwhile, Spanish monks were able to breed canaries in their monasteries. They sold canaries throughout Spain, as well as in Italy, France, and England. To eliminate competition, they sold only males. This situation lasted for almost a hundred years until some female canaries somehow showed up in Italy. By 1600, canaries were being bred in Italy, and the first variations were developed. Soon canary breeding spread to England, France, and Holland.

Once canaries made their way to Germany, miners in Tyrol, an alpine region in western Austria and northern Italy, decided to breed canaries as a way to make some extra money. They not only developed new color variations but were also able to improve the canary's singing ability. They used European nightingales as tutors to teach the male canaries to imitate their beautiful song. The best singers were the most expensive canaries. The canary's popularity reached an all-time high by the eighteenth century.

In the nineteenth century many miners from Tyrol moved to the Harz Mountains in central Germany to look for work. They brought their canaries along with them and started to breed the birds there. The canaries learned a new type of song from the rolling waterfalls above the mines, and soon the Harz Roller breed was born. Harz Rollers are still the best-known song canaries.

CANARIES AS PETS

We usually picture canaries as small yellow birds, but selective breeding has produced many different colors, body types, and even singing voices. Today there are three main types of canaries: song canaries (bred for their singing voices), color-bred (bred for their colors), and type canaries (bred for their body length, wing shape, and other features). These birds may vary greatly in size, from 4.3 to 9 inches (11 to 23 cm), depending on the type. Wild canaries are an average of 4.9 inches (12.5 cm) long.

Many people like to keep canaries for their sweet songs, but you don't always know what you're getting when you buy one from a pet store. If you want a singing canary, you should get a male. Some females sing, but their song is not as pleasant or varied as a male's. But males and females are hard to tell apart. Another problem is that you may get a color-bred or type canary instead. These birds can sing, but their voices won't be as sweet-sounding as song canaries. If you are looking at canaries in a pet store, you could listen to the canaries sing and choose one that sounds good to you. Or you could buy a canary from a breeder, who is probably more familiar with the canaries than most pet store employees.

Canaries are not as easy to tame as budgies. They also don't usually form a close bond with their owners. With patience, however, canaries can be trained to perch on your finger or arm.

Canaries tend to be rather shy and nervous and should not be housed with aggressive birds, such as budgies and parakeets. But they can be housed with other kinds of finches. Male canaries should not be kept together in a small cage or they will fight. However, there shouldn't be any problems if the cage is large enough and the males are able to establish their own territories. Females are more social than males and can be kept together. (But remember, the females won't sing, although they will make soft, chirping sounds.)

INTERNET RESOURCES

www.aviannetwork.com/canaries/ "Canaries"

www.bellaonline.com/articles/art4176.asp "All the Songs From the Heavens All in One Pet Canary" by Diana Geiger

www.exotictropicals.com/encyclo/birds/canaries/CanaryProfile.htm "All About Canaries at Animal-World.com"

www.petbird.com/faq/canary.htm "Pet Bird Canary FAQ"

FAST FACTS

Scientific name	*Gallus domesticus* (domestic chicken) in Family Phasianidae
Cost	$1 or more for show quality
Food	Chicken feed (sold in pet or feed stores); scratch can be given as a treat.
Housing	Outdoor coop or structure 8 by 12 feet (about 250 by 350 cm) is good for thirty large chickens or fifty bantams. Coop should include nest boxes for each chicken lined with wood shavings, straw, sawdust, or other absorbent material. Add a thick layer of this "litter" on the floor as well, to keep the coop from smelling bad. Also provide a few perches, a feeder, and water dishes. Chickens should be kept in a fenced-in area during the day and locked in their coop at night to protect them from nighttime predators.
Training	Can be trained to come when you call it; can learn to eat from your hand; can be held and petted.
Special Notes	Check local zoning regulations for keeping chickens. Many cities and towns do not allow farm animals, even single pets.

CHICKEN

WHEN MOST PEOPLE THINK OF chickens, they think of something to eat, rather than a pet. Chickens have been raised for food for thousands of years. Today, many people also raise chickens as a hobby, and breeders have created many unusual varieties that win prizes at pet shows.

Raising chickens can be a lot of work, but it can be fun, too. These birds are smarter than you might think and can learn to do tricks. And what other pet can supply you with eggs for breakfast?

What's in a Name?

Chicken is a general term used to describe both males and females. A female chicken is called a hen, and a male chicken is a rooster or cock. A young female, under a year, is called a pullet; a young male is a cockerel.

THE CHICKEN'S WILD WAYS

Chickens have been domesticated for five thousand years. All of today's breeds and varieties are descendants of the red jungle fowl from Southeast Asia, where they are still found in the wild. People first raised chickens in India as early as 3200 B.C. They were easy to tame because the chickens liked to stay in one place. People fed them and built little "houses" to attract wild chickens. These chicken coops had all the comforts of home: a wood perch for roosting and nests for laying eggs. The chickens were protected from predators, and they provided a regular supply of eggs.

The first domesticated chickens were too scrawny to be used for food. They were used mainly for cockfighting, a spectator sport that involved a fight between two roosters. Over the years, people started to breed chickens, choosing the biggest ones for meat and the best egg-layers for eggs. Later, people bread unusual varieties as pets. By the eighteenth century, chickens were shown in exhibitions in Europe.

Even after thousands of years of domestication, chickens still have many instincts from their wild ancestors. In the wild, red jungle fowl live in flocks. During the day, they peck the ground for insects and seeds to eat. At night, these wild chickens roost together in trees, usually in the same location night after night. Chickens are not known for their flying abilities, but they can fly short distances to get up a tree or escape from enemies.

What Happens in a Chicken's Innards?

The seeds that a chicken eats are stored at first in its crop. Digestion takes place in a two-part stomach. The first part adds digestive juices. The second part, the gizzard, mixes and grinds the food. Like other birds, chickens swallow sand or small stones that help to grind the food in the gizzard.

A flock is usually made up of a rooster, several hens, and some immature birds. The chickens in a flock sort themselves out into a "pecking order." Each chicken knows its place in the group and pecks those of lower social status. The rooster is usually the leader of the group. He is very territorial and crows loudly to let other chickens in the area know the limits of his flock's territory. The rooster also guards the flock against predators such as hawks, foxes, rats, cats, and dogs. When the flock is threatened he crows a warning, and the other chickens quickly run for cover. The rooster ruffles his neck feathers to make himself look bigger and meaner. If necessary, he may attack the predator with his beak, claws, and the bony "spurs" on his legs.

Fighting may also occur within a flock. Sometimes chickens argue over their rank in the pecking order, especially when a new member joins the flock. The two challengers stare at each other for several minutes until one of them backs down.

A rooster may mate with three to five hens. When a hen is ready to lay an egg, she sends out a mating call to get the rooster's attention. The pair pick out a nesting site and gather twigs, feathers, leaves, and loose dirt for the nest, which is a shallow hole scraped in the ground. As the hen lays an egg, she makes a loud cackle sound, then she and the rooster return to the flock. She will lay another egg each day, until she has enough to start brooding—sitting on the eggs to keep them warm for about three weeks, until the chicks hatch. The down-covered chicks can walk around and peck for seeds right away, but they still snuggle under their mother for warmth.

It's hard to tell the sexes apart at first, but as they grow, differences become obvious. All chickens have a red, fleshy growth on their heads called a *comb*. They also have two red-colored *wattles* that dangle from their chin. A rooster's comb and wattle are larger and redder than those of a hen.

CHICKENS AS PETS

Chickens have come a long way since they were first domesticated long ago. Selective breeding has produced some of the most unusual looking chickens imaginable. Some chickens have feathers growing on their legs and feet. (Most chickens' legs and feet are bare.) Some kinds have a crest of feathers on their head. There are also chickens with feathers on the sides of their face or a "beard" of feathers under their chin.

The many breeds and varieties of chickens are classified as either large or bantam. A bantam is a miniature chicken. It is about a quarter of the size of a regular chicken. Bantams are probably a better choice for a pet because of their small size.

How many chickens should you get? Should you get hens and a rooster, too? Since chickens are social animals, it is a good idea to get at least two. You don't need to get a rooster unless you want to breed them. (Hens don't need roosters to lay eggs for eating.) Some people keep roosters because they make good "watchdogs" and help to protect the hens, but roosters may annoy neighbors with their loud crowing. And they don't crow only at sunrise; they may crow any time during the day and even sometimes at night.

Chickens can become gentle and tame if they are handled often when they are young. Instead of scurrying away when you approach them, they will let you pick them up and pet them. They can even learn to recognize their names and come when you call them.

Some people allow their chickens to roam freely. This is a good way for them to balance their diet by eating leaves, seeds, and insects. But they can do a lot of damage to a lawn by digging it up with their strong claws and beak. They may also be in danger from predators or traffic on nearby roads. It is best to keep your chickens in a large fenced-in area surrounding their coop, where they can go to seek shelter.

INTERNET RESOURCES

www.afn.org/~poultry/egghen.htm "How a Hen Lays Her Egg" by Wiebe H. van der Molen

www.amplyta.com/ "Welcome to The American Poultry Association"

www.i4at.org/lib2/chickens.htm "Raising Chickens"

www.upc-online.org/stories/chcken_talk.html "Chicken Talk" by Karen Davis, Ph.D.

www.upc-online.org/cockfighting/foragers.html "Chickens Are Foragers, Not Fighters" by Karen Davis, Ph.D.

FAST FACTS

Scientific name	*Columba livia* (domestic or common pigeon) in Family Columbidae
Cost	$10 up to hundreds of dollars for show quality
Food	Pigeon feed (mixture of seeds and grains sold in feed stores); diet may also include vegetation, such as lettuce (not iceberg); dry or frozen green peas, crushed peanuts, and a mineral grit mixture (but not chicken grit).
Housing	An outdoor coop or hutch mounted on a wall or pole, at least 26 inches (67 cm) wide, 18 to 20 inches (46 to 51 cm) deep, and 16 inches (41 cm) high for a pair. Should provide protection from drafts and include nest compartments, perches, and food and water bowls.
Training	Can be trained to eat from your hand. Special techniques can be used to teach pigeons to "home." They are usually taught in groups.
Special Notes	Check with your local wildlife agencies for local regulations on keeping pigeons.

PIGEON

WHEN YOU THINK OF PIGEONS, you probably picture
a flock of birds in the city park leaving droppings as they search the ground for
bread crumbs, popcorn, and other tasty tidbits that people left behind.

It's fun to feed the pigeons in the park, but they are not the kind of bird you
can take home as a pet. There are many other kinds of pigeons, and some of
them are raised by people. Carrier pigeons have been used for thousands of years
to carry messages. Racing pigeons provide sports entertainment. A variety of fancy
pigeons are bred for their looks and take prizes at pigeon shows.

A SEMI-WILD LIFE

The pigeons that flock in the city are not domesticated, but they're not exactly
wild, either. They are feral, meaning that they are former pets that are now living on their own. Today's pigeons, both feral and domesticated, are descendants
of the wild rock dove, which used to be found throughout Europe, Asia, and
northern Africa.

Pigeon or Dove?

*Pigeons and doves are actually the same, biologically. The larger birds are usual-
ly called pigeons, and the smaller species are called doves. Interestingly, people tend
to value doves and view them as a symbol of peace and love, but pigeons are not
as well-liked.*

There are almost three hundred species of pigeons and doves in the world.
Most of them live in the tropics, but their habitats vary greatly from the humid
rain forest to the dry desert, to the temperate regions of Europe and North America. No matter where they live, all pigeons share the same basic behaviors for sur-
vival in the wild.

Pigeons live together in large flocks, whether they are roosting or looking for
food and water. Large numbers of birds search the ground for seeds, grains, nuts,
and berries. They may also eat insects and snails. Pigeons drink a lot of water,

but they don't sip it up and tilt their head back as many other birds do. Instead, they stick their beaks into the water and suck it up as if they were using a straw.

Pigeons depend on safety in numbers to protect them from their enemies, such as cats, hawks, falcons, owls, or even rats. If a predator threatens the flock, the pigeons quickly take to the air, with a thundering sound of their beating wings.

When the breeding season arrives, the males leave the flock to look for a good nesting site in a tree. When a male has found just the right spot, he starts to coo softly to attract a mate. Then he struts around and bobs his head. A female bobs her head, too, to show the male that she's interested. The male continues to coo as he lifts his wings, spreads his tail, and dances around her. Then they rub their beaks together, and the two birds become an official "couple," a pairing that will last for the rest of their lives.

During the courtship, the male pigeon feeds his mate by letting her stick her beak into his mouth and eat partly digested, regurgitated food, much like the way adults feed their young. After about a week of courting, the two birds mate. The female then waits in the nesting site, while the male collects small twigs, roots, grass, straw, and feathers for the nest. The male gives his mate the materials, and she builds the nest by herself. When she's done, the female lays two eggs, two days apart. But she doesn't start sitting on them until the second egg is laid. That way both will hatch at the same time.

Both parents take turns sitting on the eggs—the male from mid-morning until late afternoon, and the female the rest of the time. The eggs hatch in about eighteen to nineteen days. After about thirty days, the young birds are ready to leave the nest. The parents may continue to feed them for another week or two.

Pigeon Milk

For the first few days of life, baby pigeons are fed pigeon milk by both parents. Pigeon milk is a cheeselike substance produced inside the crops of both parents and put into the mouths of the chicks. After a few days, the pigeon milk is mixed with grains and seeds.

PIGEONS IN HISTORY

Pigeons were first raised by Egyptians for food as early as 2600 B.C. Later the Romans used pigeons for food as well, but soon discovered that they were useful messengers. Pigeons have an amazing homing ability; they can find their way back home, even when they are taken to places they have never been before. In A.D. 1150, the sultan of Baghdad started a pigeon postal service that continued until 1258. These carrier pigeons were able to carry important messages, packages, and medicines over rough terrain.

Carrier pigeons have played an important part in history, especially during wartime. In fact, pigeons have saved hundreds of lives. They were used by the U.S. military during World War I, World War II, and the Korean War, and delivered thousands of messages from the front lines to the command center. Pigeons replaced communication by radio, which often did not work because it was damaged or out of transmission range. Sometimes pigeons were fitted with cameras that took pictures of enemy troops.

> **DID YOU KNOW?**
> Scientists believe that pigeons have a magnetic substance in their brains that can detect the Earth's magnetic field and use it to navigate, somewhat like a compass.

Carrier pigeons are no longer used to carry messages in most parts of the world. But many people keep pigeons as pets and have turned their remarkable homing instincts into a hobby.

PIGEONS AS PETS

From the original wild rock dove ancestors, there are now more than two hundred breeds of domesticated pigeons. There are three main categories: homing (carrier) pigeons, rollers and tumblers (performance pigeons), and fancy or exhibition (show) pigeons.

Many people around the world raise homing pigeons and train them to race in competitions. (Pigeon racing is a national sport in Belgium.) Pigeons are released in unfamiliar places, up to 500 miles (805 km) away, and the first bird to make it home wins the race. Racing pigeons fly at an average speed of 50 miles (80 km) per hour.

Rollers and tumblers are pigeons that do acrobatic stunts. Rollers can spin around in the air and do backward and forward somersaults while they are flying. Tumblers do somersaults when they are dropped.

The third group of pigeons is bred for show competitions. These breeds vary greatly in appearance. The fantail has a large breast and extra tail feathers—thirty to thirty-two, compared with the usual twelve to fourteen tail feathers. Jacobins have a large feathered crest covering their head. Pouters and croppers have heavy feathering on their feet, and they can inflate their breasts so that they look very large. Domesticated pigeons can live for up to fifteen to twenty years.

INTERNET RESOURCES

members.aol.com/duiven/highlight/highligh.htm "The Pigeon Cote: Breed Showcase"

www.angelfire.com/ga3/pigeongenetics/BASICPIGEONINFO.html "Basic Pigeon Information" by Frank Mosca

www.angfelfire.com/ks/rollerpigeon/generalcare.html "Basic Care and Breeding of Pigeons"

FAST FACTS

Scientific name	*Pavo cristatus* (Indian blue peafowl) in Family Phasianidae
Cost	$15 and up
Food	Game bird feed and cracked corn, dry cat food, sweet corn, apples, lettuce, clover, and dandelion leaves
Housing	Free roaming, or fenced-in area with wire or net covering at least 6 feet (1.8 m) high and 10 feet (3 m) wide. There should also be a covered structure to protect the bird from bad weather conditions. Roosting sites, such as a tree or other tall object, should be available, as well as food and water bowls.
Training	May be trained to eat from your hand.
Special Notes	Check with your local wildlife agencies for local regulations on keeping peacocks.

PEACOCK

A PEACOCK STRUTTING AROUND and spreading his long, beautiful feathers is a spectacular sight. You may have seen peacocks showing off at a zoo, a farm, or even someone's backyard. Peacocks are one of the most beautiful birds in the world, but these brightly colored birds are actually all males. Females are called *peahens*. Males and females together are *peafowl*. But most people tend to call these birds peacocks, no matter what their sex.

A PEACOCK'S LIFE

Peacocks are originally from Southeast Asia, but over the years they have been introduced to many parts of the world, including North America. The best-known species is the Indian blue peafowl, native to India and Sri Lanka. The peacock is the national bird of India.

The Indian peacock has a shimmering bluish-green neck and breast and a train of greenish feathers, each one marked with a circle that resembles an eye. The peacock is 3 to 4.5 feet (91 to 137 cm) long, plus a 4- to 5-foot (122- to 152-cm) train. The train, made up of 100 to150 feathers, is commonly called the tail, but it is not the bird's tail. It covers the real tail, which consists of twenty much smaller, brown feathers. The tail feathers help to support the long train when the peacock lifts it up or moves it around. The peahen is slightly smaller than the male, 2.5 to 3.5 feet (76 to 107 cm) long. She does not have a train and has brown feathers instead of the bright colors of the male. Both sexes have short-feathered crests on their heads, although the peacock's is more colorful.

> ### DID YOU KNOW?
> Peacocks are the largest members of the pheasant family, which also includes quails, partridges, and jungle fowl. All male pheasants have long, colorful feathers.

In the wild, peafowl are usually found in open lowland forests near the water. They live together in flocks. During the day, the flock spends a lot of time on the ground, searching for various things to eat, such as seeds, fruits, plants, insects, and even mice and snakes. They help to cut down the cobra population in India by eating the young snakes.

When it's time to rest, the flocks roost in tall trees, making it easier to watch for predators, such as wolves, coyotes, foxes, hawks, and large owls. Peafowl communicate through rather harsh calls. If one of the birds feels threatened, it will give off loud shrieking cries to warn the others. These birds are not the best fliers, but they can fly quickly over short distances. If they have to, they can dive into a bush to escape a hungry hawk or fly up to a tall tree branch to flee from a fox.

The peacock's beautiful feathers have one main purpose: to attract females. Unlike many other birds, peacocks do not look for just one mate. A peacock may mate with as many as five females. These peahens, known as a harem, become a part of the peacock's family, in which he is the head of the household.

In the spring, the peacock gets ready to start his family. He stakes out his territory and will fight other males for the peahens, if necessary. Peacocks have very sharp spurs on their legs and use their legs to fight. The peacock sends out a mating call that sounds much like a mewing cat. But this "cat's meow" is very loud—it can be heard up to 2 miles (3 km) away! The peacock spreads out his spectacular train of feathers like a fan, sticking them straight up in the air, as he leans his body slightly forward to display them. The feathers seem to shimmer in the light, showing off an array of blues, greens, violets, reds, oranges, and yellows. The peacock struts around, moving his body from side to side. He may also get his mates' attention by shaking his feathers to make a rattling sound. If the peahens liked the show, they will become a part of the peacock's harem.

Peahens don't build nests. They simply scratch out a shallow hole in the ground, usually in a secluded location, hidden from predators. They line their "nest" with some leaves and a few sticks. The female may lay from three to twelve eggs, although four to six is the average. The female takes care of the eggs by herself. The peacock does not take turns sitting on them.

After twenty-eight days, the eggs are ready to hatch, and baby peachicks emerge. Peachicks are born with their flight feathers and can fly within a week or two. The mother tries to get her young to fly up into the trees as soon as possible so they won't be eaten by predators. At about two weeks of age, peachicks can fly to branches that are 3 feet (1 m) high. The mother teaches her chicks how to look for food, such as small insects and berries. After nine weeks, the young peafowl are ready to live on their own. It takes up to three years for the peacock's train to come in fully. He molts his train every year after the breeding season. After each molt, the train may become longer and fuller until the peacock is five or six years old.

PEACOCKS AS PETS

What would it be like to own such an exotic animal as a peacock? Its beautiful feathers would attract family and friends, and you could be the talk of the town. Unfortunately, these birds do not sound as beautiful as they look. Peacocks are especially noisy during the breeding season. They will make loud calls, day and night. This will not make you very popular around the neighborhood.

Peacocks often stay close to home if they are allowed to roam freely, as long as they are provided with food and shelter. However, neighbors may not like a visiting peacock leaving droppings or damaging their flower or vegetable gardens.

Peacocks can be kept in a fenced-in area, but they need a lot of room to move around, especially when they spread out their feathers. Their pen should be covered with wire or netting so they won't fly out of it. They also need a place to roost, which can be a tree or some other structure. (Free-roaming peacocks have been known to sit on top of people's houses.) There should also be some kind of shelter to protect them from cold temperatures or bad weather.

Keeping peacocks as pets is not for everyone. If you like these birds for their beauty, it's probably best to watch them at a zoo or farm. They are a big responsibility and should be left to experienced bird keepers.

INTERNET RESOURCES

gaga.essortment.com/peacocks_rkbn.htm "Facts About Peacocks"

peacockgirl.tripod.com/Peafowl_Info/General_Infox.html "Peafowl General Information"

wildwnc.org/af/peafowl.html "Indian Peafowl"

www.gamebird.com/peacock.html "The Peacock Information Page: All About Peafowl!"

FAST FACTS

Scientific name	*Ramphastos toco* (toco toucan); *R. tucanus* (red bill toucan); *R. sulfuratus* (keel bill toucan); *R. vitellinus* (channel bill toucan); in Family Ramphastidae
Cost	$750 up to $8,000 for toco toucans
Food	Mostly fruit, such as papayas, grapes, cantaloupe, apples, and bananas. Do not give citric fruits, such as grapefruit, oranges, lime, pineapple, and tomato, which have a high acid content. Also, toucans are prone to an iron storage disease, in which iron builds up in the body. Supplement fruit diet with Mazuri Low Iron Softbill diet (available in pet or feed stores).
Housing	Large cage at least 4 by 8 by 4 feet (1.2 x 2.4 x 1.2 m) for smaller birds; 8 by 12 by 8 feet (2.4 x 3.6 x 2.4 m) for average-size birds. Provide perches of different sizes and textures, as well as food and water bottle.
Training	May be trained to perch on your arm. If you let them perch on your shoulder, they may become too dominant. May learn to play catch or roll over.
Special Notes	Check with your local wildlife agencies for local regulations on keeping toucans.

TOUCAN

YOU'VE PROBABLY SEEN THAT brightly colored bird with a big bill in TV ads and on cereal boxes. It looks like something dreamed up by a cartoonist, but it's copied from a real bird, the toucan.

Toucans look somewhat like parrots, but they belong to a different family. These big birds can't talk like the one in the TV commercial, but they are just as smart as parrots and can be trained to do tricks. They also make great companions because they can be very friendly and affectionate. However, toucans are very expensive, some costing thousands of dollars.

TOUCANS IN THE WILD

Toucans are large tropical birds that live in South and Central America. Most of them can be found in lowland rain forests, although some species live in the mountains, as high as 9,000 feet (2,743 m) above sea level. They spend much of their lives sitting on the treetops of the forest canopy. Some of these trees may be 150 feet (46 m) tall! Toucans are not great fliers because of their large beaks, short wings, and heavy, chunky bodies. They usually prefer to hop from branch to branch. They can fly short distances, though.

Toucans belong to a group of birds called softbills. Their bills (or beaks) are not really soft, but they're not really hard, either. Softbills can't use their bills to crack open nuts the way parrots can, or carve out a nesting hole in sturdy bark. The toucan's beak is very long—in some cases almost as long as its entire body. It looks heavy, but it's actually very light because it has an airy, honeycomb structure inside.

Toucans love to eat fruit. They have a lot to choose from in the rain forest, where there may be hundreds of different kinds. Often the fruit grows on long thin branches, which might crack if a toucan sat on them. So the stocky bird sits on a thick, sturdy branch that can handle its weight and uses its long bill to pick off fruits and berries from the thinner branches. Toothlike ridges along the edges of the bill help to saw the soft fruit into chunks. Then the bird flips its head back, tosses a chunk of food into the air and catches it in its mouth. Its featherlike tongue moves the food along like a conveyor belt, down into its throat.

Toucans don't drink a lot of water because they get the moisture they need from the fruit they eat. Sometimes they add a little protein to their diet by eating insects, spiders, and even lizards, snakes, eggs, or baby birds.

43

Toucans are sociable birds and live in small groups. They eat, rest, and play together. They love to play games, such as tossing food to one another or wrestling with their beaks. One toucan will try to knock the other off a branch.

The toucan's brightly colored bill acts as camouflage. During the day, hungry eagles or hawks are unlikely to notice the colorful toucans among the tropical flowers and fruits—unless their loud chattering gives them away. At night a toucan lays its beak over its back and folds its dark tail over the beak, hiding its colors. This helps to hide the sleeping bird from night stalkers.

Toucans can identify individuals by the markings on their bills. They wave their bills to scare off smaller birds, to defend a territory, or to signal to a potential mate. When a male wants to attract a mate, he swings his bill up and down.

As a part of the mating ritual, the two birds start to hit each other with their bills or may throw food at each other. Like many other birds, toucans usually form close bonds with their mates, which last for a lifetime.

Toucans nest high above the ground in tree cavities made by woodpeckers or parrots. If the hole is too small for the toucan couple, they both help to make it bigger by using their bills to remove soft bits of rotted wood. The female lays two to four eggs on the floor of the nesting cavity. She may cushion the nest with some regurgitated seeds. The male and female take turns keeping the eggs warm. If the eggs are threatened, though, the parents have to fly away to safety because they are no match for predators. If they stayed, they would be killed.

In about fifteen to sixteen days, the eggs are ready to hatch. Baby toucans are born blind and without feathers. Their eyes don't open until they are three weeks old, and they don't get all their feathers until about seven or eight weeks. Soon they will be able to fly away from the nest, but they will still need their parents' care for a little while longer.

TOUCANS AS PETS

The toucan on Fruit Loops cereal boxes is a keel bill toucan. These birds are sold as pets, but the most popular species is the toco toucan. The toco is the largest of all the toucans and may grow up to 25 inches (64 cm) long. It has a black body with a white "bib" on its chest and a bright orange beak with a black spot at the end.

Toucans can become friendly and affectionate when they are tamed at a young age. They love attention and like to be petted or scratched. If the bird feels comfortable and at home, it will sit happily on your arm or shoulder. (But don't encourage a habit of shoulder perching, which may make the bird too dominant.) Toucans are very playful and smart. They have even been stars in bird shows. They can learn to play catch with a piece of fruit or a small ball. They may also learn to roll over. Some people have trained their toucan pets to eliminate body wastes only in their cage.

Toucans can be loud at times, making chattering or croaking sounds. These birds are not nearly as noisy as some parrots, though.

Toucans need a lot of room to spread their wings, and they should be allowed to exercise outside the cage. Fortunately, toucans cannot cause the kind of damage that parrots can. The muscles in their bill are too weak to rip apart furniture or other household items. They should be watched carefully, though, so that they don't get injured.

Toucans should not be kept in the same cage with smaller birds or other bird species. They will fight and may even kill other birds.

Mini-Toucan Pet

If you like the way the toucan looks, but you can't spare the room for such a large bird, you might want to consider getting a toucanet. This "mini-toucan," 13 to 14 inches (33 to 36 cm) long, looks like a smaller version of a toucan. It may be more nervous than a toucan, though.

INTERNET RESOURCES

www.birdtimes.com/breeds/toucan.shtml "The Toucan: The Bill with a Bird" by Antoinette Templet

www.emeraldforestbirds.com/efbgtcs.htm "Emerald Forest Bird Gardens Care Sheet"

www.pet-net.net/pet_birds/toucans.htm "About Toucans"

NOT A PET!

Each Easter, thousands of wide-eyed children receive gifts of chicks or ducklings, symbols of nature's rebirth in the spring. These cute little balls of fluff are not toys, and they are not a very good choice as pets—unless you live on a farm. The young owners soon find that birds can be messy, noisy, and a big responsibility. Within a few weeks, chicks and ducklings are being taken to animal shelters, and many more are dropped off in the woods to "go back to the wild" (where they are unlikely to survive) or die because their new owners did not know how to care for them properly.

A lot of people don't realize how much time and affection a pet bird needs to live as a contented member of the family. They may not have "done their homework" beforehand, to find out the habits of the birds and their special needs. If you need peace and quiet, you would not be happy with a screeching macaw or cockatoo, and even the sweet songs of a canary might be more than you can handle. People who live in an apartment would not have room for a large parrot or a toucan; budgies, lovebirds, or canaries would be a more practical choice. You might dream of having a bird who can talk to you, but could you cope with other typical habits of a parrot? These birds can be very demanding.

Harry Potter fans may think it would be cool to have a pet owl, but raptors (hunting birds) are not good pet choices. A snowy owl like Harry's Hedwig, for example, needs plenty of room to fly. Even an aviary would be too cramped. Young owls are cute and smart, but they are not domesticated animals and keep their wild instincts. As birds of prey, their eating habits are pretty gross by human standards. Some birds of prey, such as falcons, have been tamed and kept as hunting companions for thousands of years. But raptors are dangerous pets, unsuitable for all but experienced owners.

Moreover, many raptor species are endangered in the wild, regulated by strict laws. In the United States, it is illegal to capture or own an owl (or even a single owl feather!) without special permits. Many popular pet bird species are also endangered—partly because they are so popular. Close to a million parrots are exported from their native countries each year for the pet trade, and far larger numbers are smuggled out illegally. This is a billion-dollar business! Cruel and wasteful methods may be used to capture them. Buying only captive-bred birds can help to protect the wild populations.

So what do you do if you find that you and your new pet bird simply can't get along? You have a responsibility to help it find a more suitable home. (Remember, many birds can live a long time—some as long as people!) Bird rescue organizations nurse birds that have been abused back to health; provide information and advice for pet owners who are having problems; and carefully screen people who would like to adopt a "used bird." To find a reputable bird rescue organization near you, check the Bird Placement Program Web site (**www.avi-sci.com/bpp**) or call (330) 722-1627.

FOR FURTHER INFORMATION

Note: Before attempting to keep a kind of pet that is new to you, it is a good idea to read one or more pet manuals about that species or breed. Check your local library, pet shop, or bookstore. Search for information on the species or breed on the Internet.

BOOKS

Alderton, David. *The Ultimate Encyclopedia of Caged and Aviary Birds.* New York: Lorenz Books, 2000.

Alderton, David. *You & Your Pet Bird.* New York: Alfred A. Knopf, 2001.

Burgmann, Petra M. *Feeding Your Pet Bird.* New York: Barrons Educational Series, 1993.

Dorge, Ray, and Gail Sibley. *A Guide to . . . Pet & Companion Birds: Their Keeping, Training & Well-Being.* Australia: ABK Publications, 1998.

Evans, Mark, and Roger A. Caras. *Birds (ASPCA Pet Care Guides for Kids).* New York: Dorling Kindersley, 2001.

Gallerstein, Gary A., and Heather Acker. *The Complete Bird Owner's Handbook.* New York: John Wiley & Sons, 1994.

INTERNET RESOURCES

mel.lib.mi.us/science/petbird.html "Pet Birds" (articles on choosing a bird and links for specific breeds, care & feeding, and training)

netvet.wustl.edu/birds.htm "Electronic Zoo: NetVet Veterinary Resources—Bird Sites" (links for poultry, pet birds, and other birds)

petplace.netscape.com/netscape/nsArtShow.asp?artID=3130 "Your Guide to Selecting a Bird" by Dr. Dawn Ruben

www.birdsnways.com/ "Birds n Ways Guide to Parrots & Exotic Pet Birds"

www.petstation.com/birds.html "BirdStation—All About Pet Birds"

www.petstation.com/whatbird.html "Which Bird for Me?" by R. R. Holster

www.upatsix.com/into.php "Pet Bird"

INDEX

Page numbers in *italics* refer to illustrations.